LIGHT OF HEAVEN

A CHILDREN'S BOOK OF SAINTS

— ADALEE HUDE —

Our Sunday Visitor
Huntington, Indiana

Our Sunday Visitor Publishing Division
Our Sunday Visitor, Inc.
200 Noll Plaza
Huntington, IN 46750
1-800-348-2440

ISBN: 978-1-68192-370-3 (Inventory No. T2209)
eISBN: 978-1-68192-371-0
LCCN: 2019936261

Cover design: Amanda Falk
Cover art: Adalee Hude/Shutterstock
Interior design: Amanda Falk
Interior art: Adalee Hude

PRINTED IN THE UNITED STATES OF AMERICA

PRESENTED TO

_____

BY

_____

ON

_____

To my parents, Ellen and Adrian,
who led me to the Faith, and to
my dear husband, Randy,
who helps me to live it out.

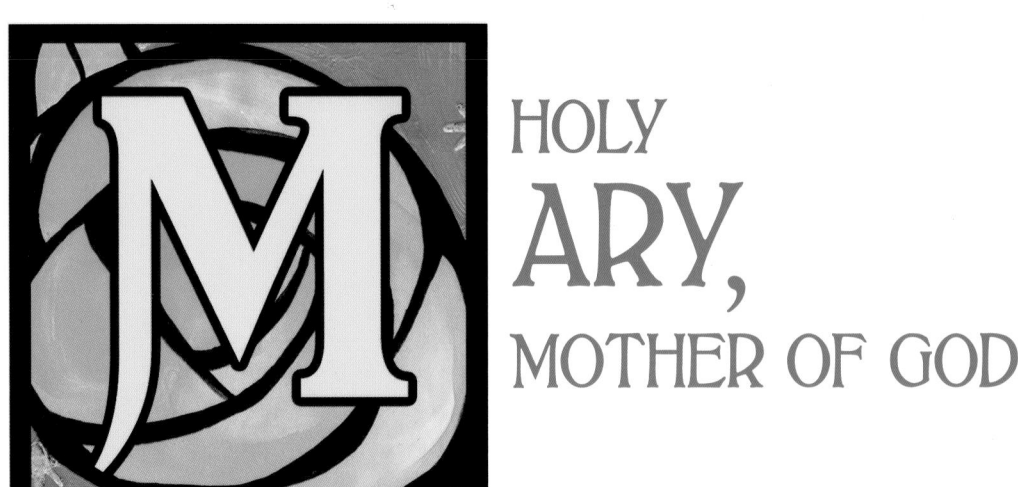

HOLY MARY, MOTHER OF GOD

***Gaudete* means "rejoice."**

Mary rejoiced in doing what God asked of her. God chose her to be the mother of his Son, Jesus. Mary said: "My soul magnifies the Lord, / and my spirit rejoices in God my Savior" (Lk 1:46–47). Mary teaches us to rejoice in God's love for us.

The Church celebrates Mary in a special way during the month of May. We also have special feast days in her honor, including January 1 (Mary, Mother of God), March 25 (the Annunciation), August 15 (the Assumption), and December 8 (the Immaculate Conception).

GAUDETE

SAINT JOSEPH

Justus means "just."

Saint Joseph was blessed by God to be the husband of Mary and the foster father of Jesus. He was a carpenter, and the Bible tells us he was "a just man" (Mt 1:19). He is the patron saint of the universal Church. He is also the patron saint of fathers, unborn children, immigrants, travelers, and workers.

Feast days: March 19 and May 1

SAINT ELIZABETH

Laetitia means "joy."

Saint Elizabeth was Mary's cousin. She was filled with joy when God gave her a baby boy, even though she was too old to have children. Her son, Saint John the Baptist, would grow up to prepare the way for Jesus.

Feast day: November 5

LAETITIA

SAINT PETER

Claves means "keys."

Saint Peter was an apostle of Jesus. Jesus chose Peter to be the leader of the Church, telling him, "I will give you the keys of the kingdom of heaven" (Mt 16:19). This meant Peter would have authority in the name of Jesus. Peter became the first pope.

Feast day: June 29

CLAVES

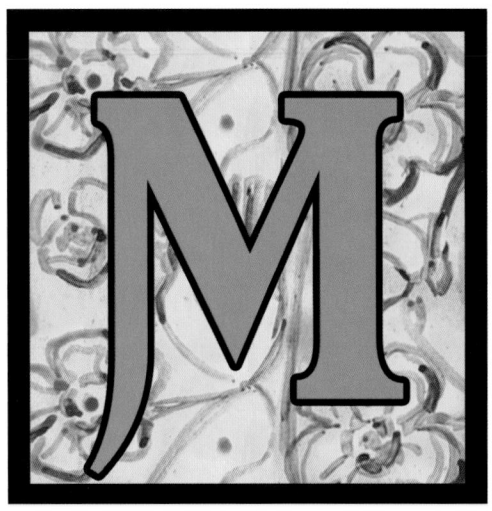

SAINT MARY MAGDALENE

Versio means "conversion."

Saint Mary Magdalene converted from a life of sin to follow Jesus. She was with Jesus at many important moments in his ministry. She was the first disciple to see him when he rose from the dead on Easter Sunday. She is the patron saint of women, hairdressers, pharmacists, and converts.

Feast day: July 22

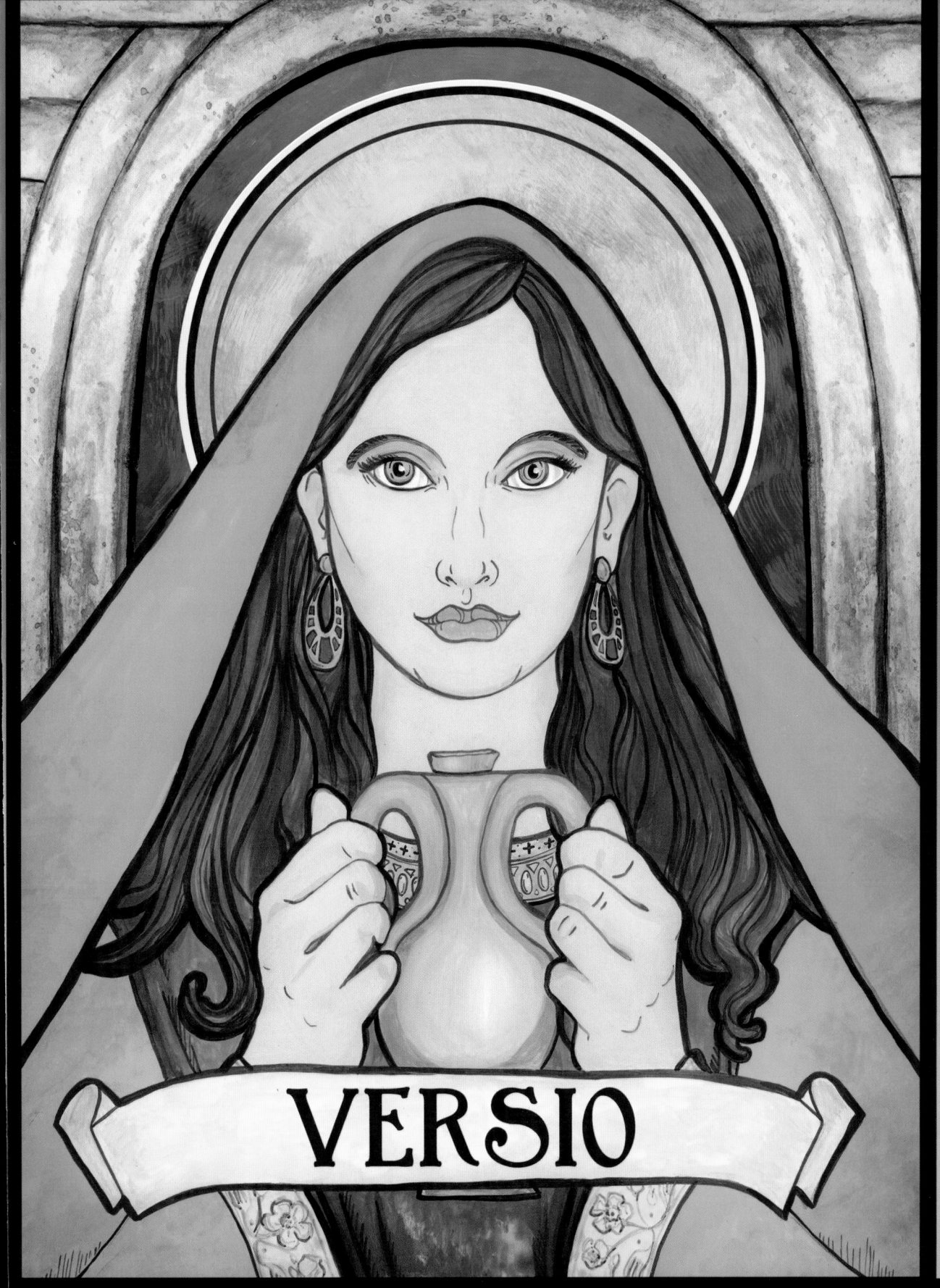

VERSIO

SAINT GEORGE

Fortitudo means "courage."

Saint George was a courageous Roman soldier who became a Christian. There is a legend that during his life he killed a dragon to save a village and brought the people to faith in Jesus. He remained faithful to Christ until the end, and he bravely died a martyr's death.

Feast day: April 23

FORTITUDO

SAINT AUGUSTINE OF HIPPO

Inquietus means "restless."

Saint Augustine was a restless young man. He wanted to find happiness in his life without God, but he was very unhappy. At last, he stopped running away from God, and he found rest. He became a bishop of the Church. He wrote many important books that help people know and love God better.

Feast day: August 28

INQUIETUS

SAINT PATRICK

Adnunciator means "preacher."

Saint Patrick was kidnapped by pirates as a young boy and taken to Ireland as a slave. Ireland was a pagan country at that time. Later, he escaped, but he had a vision that the Irish people came to him and begged him to return. He went back to Ireland and spent the rest of his life teaching the people there about God. Ireland was converted to Christianity because of his preaching.

Feast day: March 17

ADNUNCIATOR

SAINT ENEDICT

Virtus means "virtue."

Saint Benedict wanted to lead a life of great virtue. He tried to live all alone as a hermit, but God wanted him to lead other people to holiness. He became the first person in the West to organize a monastery. He and the other men who lived there were called "monks." He always told his community to live by the motto "Pray and work."

Feast day: July 11

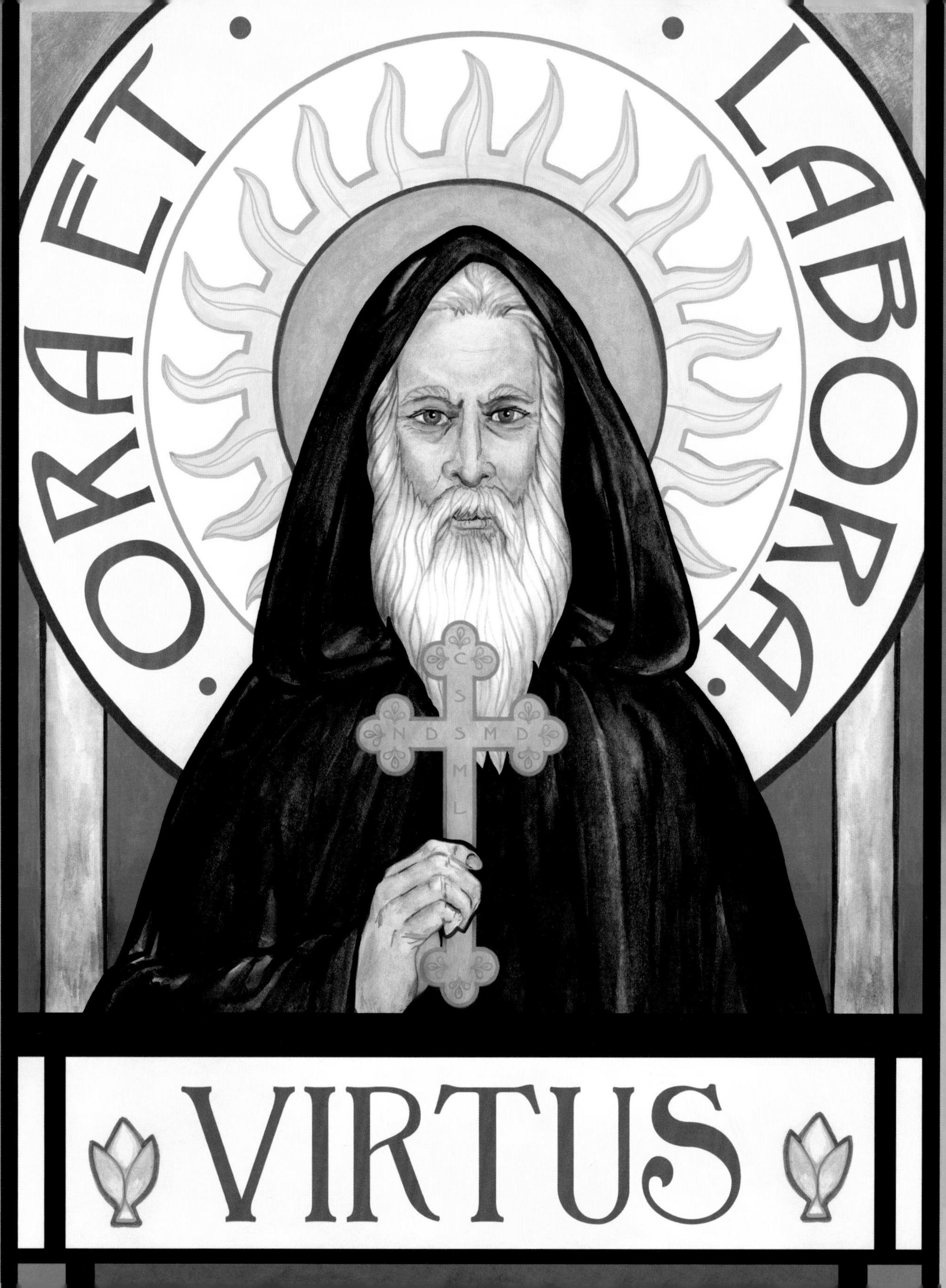

ORA ET LABORA

VIRTUS

SAINT
FRANCIS
OF ASSISI

Pax means "peace."

Saint Francis of Assisi found peace when he gave up his worldly riches and chose to live as a beggar for the Lord. He heard God calling him to rebuild the Church. He founded a religious order, the Franciscans, that exists to this day. He was also known for his love of God's creation, and he is the patron saint of animals.

Feast day: October 4

PAX

SAINT
CLARE
OF ASSISI

Lux means "light."

Saint Clare was a good friend to Saint Francis. She founded a religious order for women now known as the Poor Clares. Her name means "bright," and she shared the Light of Christ with everyone — even the raiders who tried to invade her convent. She held the Blessed Sacrament before them, and they ran away. She is the patron saint of television, because God showed her Mass on her bedroom wall when she was too ill to go to church.

Feast day: August 11

SAINT CATHERINE OF SIENA

***Ignis* means "fire."**

Saint Catherine of Siena was the youngest child of a very large family. She loved Jesus with her whole heart and gave her whole life to him. She took care of sick people, wrote letters, worked miracles, and even helped popes make important decisions. She once said: "If you are what you should be, you will set the whole world on fire."

Feast day: April 29

IGNIS

SAINT JOAN OF ARC

Valorosa **describes a brave woman.**

Saint Joan of Arc was very brave. She was only a girl when God called her to lead the army of France. She did as God asked and led the French soldiers to victory. Joan of Arc bravely died as a martyr in 1431. She is the patron saint of soldiers and of France.

Feast day: May 30

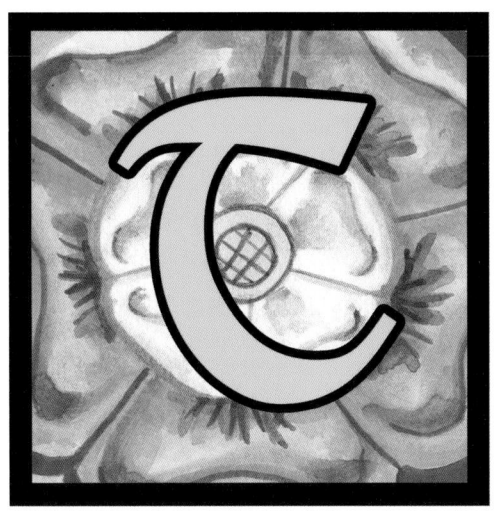

SAINT THOMAS MORE

Fidelis means "faithful."

Saint Thomas More was faithful to Jesus even when it was dangerous to be so. He was an important man in the government under King Henry VIII of England. When the king declared himself head of the church in England, Thomas More would not agree to it and returned his chain of office. The king had him killed. Thomas understood that being faithful to God must always come first, no matter what.

Feast day: June 22

FIDELIS

SAINT MARTIN DE PORRES

Humilitas means "humility."

Saint Martin de Porres was a man of great humility. He suffered many trials during his life, but he was always kind and humble. He loved to serve others. He took care of the sick and dying, worked miracles, and took special care of animals.

Feast day: November 3

HUMILITAS

SAINT
ATERI
TEKAKWITHA

Pietas means "piety."

Saint Kateri Tekakwitha was a Native American from the Mohawk tribe. She fell in love with Jesus Christ and became a Christian. She joined a community of other Native Americans who had become Christians, and she led a life of great piety. She always prayed for her people.

Feast day: July 14

SAINT HÉRÈSE OF LISIEUX

Caritas means "love."

Saint Thérèse had a heart full of love. She heard God calling her at a very young age to give her life to him. When she was fifteen years old, she became a Carmelite nun. She was known for doing little things with great love, and she called this her Little Way. When she died, she promised to send a "shower of roses" to earth from heaven out of love for us.

Feast day: October 1

CARITAS

SAINT MARIA FAUSTINA KOWALSKA

***Fiducia* means "trust."**

Saint Faustina was a Polish nun who had visions of Jesus. He wanted Faustina to teach all people to trust in his mercy. Jesus told her to have a painting made of him showing two rays coming from his heart. This painting is called the image of Divine Mercy. At the bottom are the words: "Jesus, I trust in you."

Feast day: October 5

Jesus, I Trust in You

FIDUCIA

SAINT
GIANNA
BERETTA MOLLA

Medica means "doctor."

Saint Gianna Beretta Molla was a doctor who took care of sick children. She was also a loving wife and mother. When she was pregnant with her fourth child, she learned that she might die if she gave birth to her baby. She chose to save her baby, not herself. She helps us remember the value of every human life.

Feast day: April 28

MEDICA

SAINT TERESA OF CALCUTTA

Sitio means "I thirst."

Saint Teresa of Calcutta is better known as Mother Teresa. She heard Jesus tell her: "I thirst." She knew that this was a call for her to care for the poorest of the poor. Mother Teresa always wanted to meet Jesus in others. She founded a religious order called the Missionaries of Charity.

Feast day: September 5

SITIO

SAINT JOHN PAUL II

Spes means "hope."

Pope Saint John Paul II was a man of great hope. He lived through a very difficult period of history, but he knew that we do not have to be afraid. God is always stronger than our fears. John Paul II was a wise teacher and writer. He traveled to many countries, and he helped people know the great love of God.

Feast day: October 22

SPES

ABOUT THE AUTHOR

Adalee Hude has been studying art all her life. She earned a BA in art from Cal State Long Beach. She was called from a career in secular art to focus on Catholic sacred art and writing. Her artistic repertoire includes painting, sculpture, illustration, design, and crafting. The Arts & Crafts movement, medieval art, God's beautiful world, and the lives of the saints are particular influences on her work. Follow her on Instagram @brightlyhude and on Facebook @brightlyhude. Her work is available on her website www.brightlyhude.com.